PICASSO

Cossetània EDICIONS

MALAGA

1881

Pablo Picasso is born in Malaga. His father, a drawing teacher, shows him the secrets of the profession. And soon he discovers he has an extraordinary talent. His mother doesn't understand painting, but she knows her son well. She tells him: "If you become a soldier, you'll rise to be a general. And if you become a priest, you'll be Pope." Years later, Picasso would say: "I decided to be a painter and I became Picasso."

BARCELONA

1895

His father has to move for work and the family go with him. Picasso lives in A Coruña and, some time later, in Barcelona. Of the Catalan capital, where he arrived as a teenager, he would later say: "That's where it all started." His teachers encourage him to make classical paintings, but he prefers the Bohemian lifestyle. At the 4 Gats tavern, he discovers friends and teachers, and, above all, modern painting.

BLUE PERIOD

1901-1904

On his friends' advice, Picasso wastes no time
in travelling to Paris, the capital of modern
art. It really opens the young painter's eyes.
Full of curiosity, he observes everything and
learns quickly. But his happiness doesn't last
forever... The death of his friend Casagemas
affects him deeply and influences his style.
Picasso begins to paint lonely people and
his canvases are coloured a sad blue.

ROSE PERIOD

1904-1906

In 1904, Picasso finally settles in Paris. His studio is in the Montmartre district, where he befriends other artists and falls in love with the young Fernande Olivier. At the same time, he wins a reputation as a tireless worker and restless artist. Now his pictures are distinguished by their warm shades and soft lines, with harlequins, gypsies and circus characters at the centre of them.

CUBISM

1907

In 1907 *Les demoiselles d'Avignon*
revolutionises modern art. With the portrait
of these five nude girls, Picasso invents
Cubism. It is a style influenced not only by
modern painting but also by primitive
African art. Through geometric forms, it
represents the different dimensions of reality
on a single plane. "I don't paint what I see,"
says Picasso, "I paint what I think."

YOUTH

Picasso has become one of the most important painters of his time, but he's still young and he's constantly working. Nor does he stop experimenting. Cubist landscapes fly from his brushes, but he also incorporates the collage technique. He creates the sets for the Russian ballet as well. This curiosity will never leave him. As he likes to say: "When you're young, you're young for life."

GUERNICA

1937

In 1936, the Spanish Civil War breaks out and the Republic commissions Picasso to paint a mural for the International Exhibition to be held in Paris. It isn't just any commission, it is a way of fighting for peace. The resulting work is *Guernica,* which shows the bombing of this Basque town. Never before had anything like it been painted to express the horror of war.

VALLAURIS

1947

In 1947, Picasso moves to the south of France. There he returns to the Mediterranean and enjoys a period of fulfilment in his life. He lives with Françoise Gilot, plays with his children Claude and Paloma... and, above all, he works. The dove of peace becomes a symbol of concord throughout the world and his interest in ceramics opens up new opportunities for expression. At the same time, he explores new themes, such as mythology and bullfighting.

LAS MENINAS

1957

Time has passed and Picasso has matured. But, far from remaining passive, he does what he does best: paint tirelessly. His outstanding works during this period are the tributes he pays to those he considers his masters. He dedicates series to painters like Delacroix and Degas, although the most famous series is the one devoted to Velázquez. In *Las meninas,* classical and modern art go hand in hand.

MOUGINS

1973

Now very old, Picasso knows that the time has come to take his leave. Throughout his life he has received many tributes and new generations are queuing up to praise him. To them he dedicates advice such as: "Turn off the grey in your life and turn on the colours you have inside." And he still has time to paint astonishing works, like his last self-portrait. At the age of 91 he dies at his home in Mougins.

CHRONOLOGY

1881
Born in Malaga.

1891
Moves to
A Coruña.

1895
Settles in
Barcelona.

1900
First trip
to Paris.

1937
Guernica.

1907
*Les demoiselles
d'Avignon.*

1904
Rose period.

1901
Blue period.

1949
Dove of peace.

1957
Las menines

1973
Dies in Mougins.

MAZE

Young Picasso has got lost in the streets of Montmartre.
Help him find the way back to his studio.

GALLERY OF CHARACTERS

Santiago Rusiñol

One of the main representatives of Catalan art nouveau. A painter and writer, he and Ramon Casas were the men behind the 4 Gats tavern.

Fernande Olivier

Picasso's partner during the Rose Period and Cubism. She is one of the models who appears in *Les demoiselles d'Avignon*.

Carles Casagemas

Friend of the young Picasso, he accompanied him on his first trip to Paris. His death, while still very young, influenced Picasso's Blue Period.

Gertrude Stein

American writer settled in Paris. She supported many painters and was one of the first people to buy a Picasso painting.

Georges Braque

French painter and sculptor. Together with Picasso, he was one of the initiators of Cubism. One of his most representative works is *The guitar*.

THE SEVEN DIFFERENCES

Find the seven differences between the two pictures
of Picasso's studio.

WORDSEARCH

The wordsearch below conceals seven themes related to Picasso's works.

U	A	C	O	D	R	G	Y	S	G	M	E	K	D	S
L	R	P	A	B	N	B	W	A	A	E	W	G	E	W
E	L	B	R	K	F	U	E	L	P	N	I	F	M	E
M	A	L	H	A	R	L	E	Q	U	I	N	Z	O	Z
A	N	A	H	L	O	L	P	E	A	N	O	A	I	A
D	D	C	A	W	L	S	I	U	E	A	S	W	S	B
O	S	I	T	J	P	I	N	L	E	S	Q	A	E	O
S	C	O	A	U	M	S	A	I	A	M	U	S	L	Z
E	A	G	S	A	D	U	Q	Y	P	M	I	E	L	E
L	P	W	M	E	S	M	I	G	Y	P	S	I	E	S
E	E	K	D	O	V	E	Y	Z	E	O	A	Z	S	W
K	S	Q	U	L	C	A	W	A	B	A	S	L	R	O
A	N	A	B	L	L	T	A	Z	U	O	S	Z	A	E

WHERE IS PICASSO?

The 4 Gats tavern is full of Bohemians tonight. Can you find Picasso there? You will also find four painters on tandems, three pipes that have fallen on the floor and two dancers with red stockings.

THE DOVE OF PEACE

Find the two doves of peace alike!

WHERE WAS PICASSO BORN?

In which of these cities
was Pablo Picasso born?

a) Paris.

b) Malaga.

c) Barcelona.

d) A Coruña.

31

First edition: October 2016
Second edition: September 2017

© on the text: Marià Veloy Planas
© on the illustrations: David Maynar Gálvez

© on this edition:
9 Grup Editorial
Cossetània Edicions
C/ Violeta, 6 - 43800 Valls
Tel. (34) 977 60 25 91
cossetania@cossetania.com
www.cossetania.com

Translation: Simon Berrill

Design and layout: Imatge-9, SL

Printing: Leitzaran Grafikak

ISBN: 978-84-9034-540-5

DL T 1288-2016